LEADERSHIP BEHAVIOR IMPACT ON EMPLOYEE'S LOYALTY, ENGAGEMENT AND ORGANIZATIONAL PERFORMANCE

Leadership Behavior and Employee Perception of the Organization

Raimi-Akinleye Abiodun

Author's Tranquility Press
ATLANTA, GEORGIA

Copyright © 2024 by Raimi-Akinleye Abiodun

All rights reserved. No part of this publication may be reproduced, distributed or transmitted in any form or by any means, including photocopying, recording, or other electronic or mechanical methods, without the prior written permission of the publisher, except in the case of brief quotations embodied in critical reviews and certain other noncommercial uses permitted by copyright law. For permission requests, write to the publisher, addressed "Attention: Permissions Coordinator," at the address below.

Raimi Akinleye-Abiodun/Author's Tranquility Press
3900 N Commerce Dr. Suite 300 #1255
Atlanta, GA 30344, USA
www.authorstranquilitypress.com

Ordering Information:
Quantity sales. Special discounts are available on quantity purchases by corporations, associations, and others. For details, contact the "Special Sales Department" at the address above.

Leadership Behavior Impact on Employee's Loyalty, Engagement and Organizational Performance / Raimi Akinleye-Abiodun
Hardback: 978-1-964810-61-4
Paperback: 978-1-964810-38-6
eBook: 978-1-964810-39-3

Contents

Behavior #1: Embrace and Shape the Culture of Your Organization 1
    Questions to Ask Yourself 7

Behavior #2: Use Effective Communication 9
    Questions to Ask Yourself 15

Behavior #3: Be Visible 16
    Questions to Ask Yourself 19

Behavior #4: Choose Your Words Carefully to Build Employee Pride and Association 20
    Questions to Ask Yourself 23

Behavior #5: Develop a Culture of Safety 24
    Questions to Ask Yourself 31

Behavior #6: Focus on Staff Satisfaction to Build Customer Satisfaction 32
    Questions to Ask Yourself 43

Behavior #7: Set Expectations 44
    Questions to Ask Yourself 48

Behavior #8: Promote Shared Governance 49
    Questions to Ask Yourself 55

Behavior #9: Be a Quality Leader 56
    Questions to Ask Yourself 60

Behavior #10: Embrace Diversity 61
    Questions to Ask Yourself 70

Chapter Eleven Conclusion 71

Bibliography 75

Dedication

This book is dedicated to those leaders who believe in a positive working environment and its influence on the organization's performance, and to those I have had the opportunity to lead. I appreciate their unconditional kindness and unsolicited trust.

Preface

The goal of this book is to contribute to the debate on health-care delivery by making the process of leading and managing health-care organizations much more reliable and manageable as well as less stressful. I will describe key strategies that have made leaders in other industries successful and discuss how they have been applied. I will also discuss proven methods of building a dynamic leadership team for your organization.

The book will provide you with techniques that will be helpful in fostering better working relationships with your staff and other stakeholders you do business with or interact with in your everyday functions. The book will also provide some basic leadership skills that will support horizontal communication and team building among various health-care professional subcultures present within the organization.

This book is written specifically to help health-care leaders model positive behaviors that will create a better working environment—one that can be used to create a culture that encourages innovation and risk taking by employees. Whether you are managing a unit or a department or are in charge of the organization as chief executive officer, your people are looking for behaviors that they can relate to and model in their own daily activities.

In their 1974 study (reported by Robert J. House in "Path-Goal Theory of Leadership: Lessons, Legacy, and a Reformulated Theory"), House and Mitchell defined four kinds of behaviors that are highly significant for leadership success. These behaviors are needed to bring about employee engagement and satisfaction. The four types of behavior are: directive clarifying leader behavior, supportive leader behavior, participative leader behavior, and achievement-oriented behavior. Let us look at each one of these behaviors and see how they are related to the ten behaviors that this book is describing as key behaviors for motivation, loyalty, and performance.

Directive clarifying leader behavior is one that is directed toward followers' expectations. This type of behavior can be used to give specific guidance and clarifying policies, rules, and procedures. This behavior can also be used to reduce followers' role ambiguity and to clarify followers' perceptions concerning the degree to which their effort would result in successful performance and how this performance would be rewarded by the organization.

Supportive leader behavior is directed toward the satisfaction of followers' needs and preferences. This is seen when a leader shows concern for followers' welfare and attempts to create a friendly and psychologically supportive working environment. This behavior could result in greater self-confidence and social satisfaction for followers. The result is a reduction in stress level and a complete elimination of employee frustration. The result of a leader's supportive behavior is manifested in employee performance and perception of the leader's effectiveness.

Participative leader behavior is one that encourages followers' participation in decision making and work-unit operations. This is a behavior that seeks opinions from other members of the organization. This behavior increases members' autonomy and ability to carry out their intentions leading to greater effort and performance. This behavior has a direct correlation with members' degree of commitment and satisfaction with organizational goals and direction.

Achievement-oriented behavior is mostly directed toward performance. This behavior increases and encourages excellence in performance and goal setting. It helps shape the way members view their leaders' support for their growth and development.

This behavior brings out the best in employees, making them more assertive, encouraging them to strive for higher standards of performance, and giving them more confidence in their ability to meet challenging goals.

Looking at these four types of behaviors, we see how important are the ten leadership behaviors that will be presented in this book to members' satisfaction, loyalty, and performance.

I became familiar with the health-care environment as a young boy when I used to follow my father to the hospital. I developed an interest in patient care after watching how nurses, doctors, and other health-care workers interacted with their patients—how they extended their hands of friendship and their compassionate hearts to fragile, anxious people. It was my experience in the health-care industry, as a staff nurse, a clinical manager, and a director in various health-care settings that motivated me to write this book.

I have observed leaders who were effective in how they managed and led their workers, leaders who were able to motivate and energize workers to achieve the organization's goals and objectives. Some of the views expressed in this book also came from what I learned when I was pursuing my doctorate in organization and leadership development. I learned some leadership skills that all leaders and managers need to master in order to be effective. I learned that to be effective you have to be seen by your followers as a listener and as a compassionate and caring leader. You have to be a good communicator, and you must be seen as a proactive leader rather than a reactive leader. A good leader must also be seen as someone who understands diversity and what it means to have different opinions and people around the table when trying to make decision that will affect the organization and its people.

The book offers steps that can be taken by health-care leaders when confronting unknown factors. These ten behaviors will help you master the game plan and move your healthcare setting into the future. These behaviors should serve as quick learning tools that you can refer to whenever you are facing new difficulties or new challenges.

The end-of-chapter questions are designed to serve as assessment tools to be used when you are strategically thinking of your next moves. I hope they are helpful.

Acknowledgments

I am deeply grateful to so many people who have contributed to the ideas that have made this book possible. I am grateful to all my staff, both past and present, who have allowed me to learn and grow with them. Special thanks to Chris Nemets and Lisa Harris for their unflinching support. Their words of encouragement and their belief in me provided the motivation that was needed when I was putting this book together.

Thanks also to Reva Will for her assistance, ideas, collaboration, and encouragement from the beginning.

I would like to thank my family, my wife, and especially my children, Mary, James, and Margaret, for their support and encouragement. I am also grateful to my parents for instilling in me those leadership qualities and ways of thinking that have contributed to my leadership effectiveness and successes.

This acknowledgment would not be complete if I failed to mention those leaders who trained, mentored, and developed me in my quest to be a better leader. I have learned much from their behavior and leadership styles over the past eighteen years.

My humble thanks go to the almighty God who is the author of my faith, for the blessings and the good health that I have enjoyed while putting this book together. I know that God is the source of my happiness, joy, and success.

Introduction

If you ask any health-care administrator what he or she thinks about the current state of health-care delivery, I am very sure that you will hear him or her say it is not easy because of problems associated with the demands and needs of various health-care customers and stakeholders. Most of these demands are based on expectations and frustrations that are caused by high costs, coverage issues, and access problems that are far beyond administrator's control. Stakeholders' expectations are unique to each group or association. We have expectations from the government, the community, the workers, and from regulatory agencies like The Center for Medicare and Medicaid Services and The Joint Commission. The expectations from consumers and health-care professionals are enough to cause sleepless nights for hospital administrators. Each professional association has its own professional expectations that health-care leaders must know how to meet. Failure to meet them can result in bad patient outcomes and in a damaged reputation for the organization.

The environment of care that exists today calls for health-care leaders to have management talent that is good enough to compete with the increased demands of the health-care environment. Health-care leaders are expected to demonstrate specific measurable outcomes and be skilled enough to withstand the demands originating from different sections of health-care services. Today's health-care leaders must develop a system that is strong enough to navigate an industry that is influenced by complex social and political forces. Some of these forces include a shortage of professional workers, unfair reimbursement practices, and the need to meet the expectations of regulatory bodies.

One professional group whose members exercise incredible power is the physician group. Physicians contribute significantly to the success of any health-care organization as well as to CEO productivity. They play a very significant role in the hospital, and that role has helped transform them from marginalized voices into strong and dependable partners in the healthcare community. High physician satisfaction means better quality of care, improved technology, better resources for care delivery, and communication that is dual, inclusive, and respectful. Such satisfaction can also be seen as a cumulative effect of physicians' perceptions of quality of care, competency of caregivers, and the availability of services needed by customers. Physician satisfaction may also result from what doctors are hearing from their patients when they return to their offices for follow-up to the care they received while in the hospital. Overall, the constant changes in economics, politics, social issues, and technology continue to influence stakeholders' perceptions and expectations of a CEO.

As hospital chief executive officer, you are not only supposed to meet these expectations, you are also expected to know how the culture of the organization can support these expectations. You are obligated to be aware of all those initiatives that are happening in your organization. It is your job to help create and sustain a better and safer culture for your organization. Some of your functional responsibilities as Leader are to help create a culture that supports safety, caring, and professional growth. You are also expected to demonstrate leadership skills that help institute and maintain employee engagement and develop a concrete and meaningful strategy for the organization.

The history of health-care organizations tells us that successful and effective health-care leaders need the following competencies:

- communication skills

- knowledge of relationship management
- professionalism
- leadership skills
- knowledge of the health-care system
- business skills

It is also very important for the Leader to know that strategic flexibility is an increasingly sought after competitive element in today's health-care industry and something a successful health-care leader must aspire to have if the goal is a viable organization.

Some of the yardsticks that boards of governors and directors use to measure the productivity of health-care leaders are fiscal accountability, employee encouragement, sustainable culture, and customer satisfaction. All these are parts of the soft side of hospital management that must be managed effectively by the leaders. Various leadership studies have shown that meeting the needs of employees can influence them to improve performance, meet the organization's goals, and generate interest and dedication that are needed for better working condition and workers. Therefore, it is very important for a hospital administrator to use the power of the office to recognize the role of the individual within the organization. Each stakeholder and individual within your organization has a unique role in helping the organization to meet its collective mission, vision, and goals—which means that you as the leader must be able to recognize those potential individual qualities that are beneficial and useful to the overall objectives of the organization. Your job is to create an environment in which individuals will be able to link their goals with those of the organization.

Another thing that causes headaches is the reimbursement dilemma presented by insurance companies—Medicare, Medicaid, managed care, and private insurance companies like Blue Cross Blue Shield, Aetna, and other independently owned hospital-based insurance companies. These organizations dictate what, how, and when they will pay for the services rendered to their clients. They question every bill they are asked to pay. Having them as a third layer of the health-care delivery system has not been easy for most CEOs. When you look at the history of health care, majorities of patients had insurance coverage that paid the usual and customary rates for any services and admission to the hospital. There were no negotiations between the health-care facility and the insurance plan. Physicians and health-care institutions did not need approvals for recommended admissions or procedures. Most important, there was no incentive for cost savings like we have today.

Other factors that contribute to some of the headaches of health-care delivery in the modern era are associated with demands coming from both the internal and external customers and the health-care market itself. Independently, these factors are making the job expectations of health-care executives more demanding and difficult every day. Literature on healthcare management continues to show that dealing with these multiple problems would demand health-care leaders to have a plan, a process, and a culture that will support whatever program or initiatives that have been put in place. Having no definite plan is to be compared to a farmer going into the planting season without an inclination as to what type of seeds to plant for the season. It is essential for the health-care leader to know his strengths and weaknesses, to discover whether he is a motivator, a sustainer, or a strengthener of ideas and principles that support and promote growth and development of the organization.

The ten leadership behaviors shown in the following chapters will help you, the health-care executive; promote employee engagement, loyalty, and performance in your organization.

Behavior #1:
Embrace and Shape the Culture of Your Organization

I remember when, as a young boy, I first set foot in the United States of America; everything was strange to me. I had left my parents for the first time to go to a strange place where the culture, attitudes, and way of life were completely different. I came to continue with my education. I had obtained my associate's diploma in nursing education and was about to finish my college degree in human nutrition from the University of Ibadan, a leading university in Nigeria. I was confronted with a new culture and new ways of thinking when I got here. The care environment was different from the one I had experienced back home as a registered nurse. While in Nigeria, I had been a staff nurse in one of the state hospitals caring for different types of patients.

Looking at the ceiling in my room the night of my arrival, I thought about how I was going to adapt and cope with new expectations and ways of life. There were two options for me at that time: either change my old beliefs and embrace the new culture or remain my old self. A decision was made to slowly embrace the new world but do it in such a way that the things I had grown up to believe were true were not relegated to the bottom level of the equation. I began to learn the new attitudes, behaviors, and norms of my new world. This turned out to be a brilliant idea because I was able to acclimate and adjust with few difficulties.

In the same way, a successful leader must learn to embrace and also shape the culture of her organization. A successful leader must begin by understanding the culture and values of the people within the organization. Understanding and assessing an organization's culture can mean the difference between success and failure. Culture is the way of life and how people within the organization react and behave when performing their roles as members of the organization.

I remember my days as a new director for nursing operations. I came from my previous job with high energy and deep knowledge as to how to get things done and bring people together to work toward the common goals of the organization. Also, I came into this job with the benefit of my academic knowledge and achievements. I saw no obstacles, barriers, or hindrances that could stand in the way for me to achieve my goals and creating the necessary change that this new organization needed to perform well.

I worked day and night; putting things in place and making sure that my contributions as director of nursing operations were recognized and appreciated. For seven months, there were no visible changes; people remained as resistant to change as they had been when I first arrived. The resistance came from their past experiences of being misled by various leaders.

In February of 2008, I put together an event to honor all nursing preceptors, to thank them for their efforts in helping to train our new nurses. I was shocked to see that none of the invitees showed up for this event, despite all the publicity that had been done for it. This event served as an eye-opener for me. I was able to retrace my steps and talk to and learn from the staff about how we could move on and forget whatever the past had meant to them. I used the next four months to study the new culture I was working in and come up with plans and actions that were seen as friendly by the staff.

It was after my seventh month that I sat down to think and retraced my steps to find out what I had done wrong. What I found is that I had not learned enough about the norms, values, and behaviors of my new organization. I had been operating according to my familiar culture, with the same expectations in mind. It must be remembered that I had come from a bigger organization with a different vision and mindset. Celebrating successes was ongoing, and this was well appreciated by staff nurses. In my previous organization, employee participation and involvement in decision making had been excellent staff had been involved in all decisions and event planning. This high degree of staff participation made implementation less painful on the day of an event. I think the fact that this was not the way things were done in my new organization made the staff skeptical of my plan for the event.

I reoriented myself and spent the next four months studying the new norms, values, and behaviors that were part of the culture I was now presented with. It was amazing for me to see the successes that followed this single action of getting to know my new culture and behavior.

What exactly do we mean by the term *culture*? Various scholars on organizational behavior have examined culture and its impact on organizational readiness for change. They see culture as a set of values, beliefs, and ways of thinking that are shared by members of an organization. Culture to some is like a funnel that filters the ways in which people see and understand their world. It is the undefined principle that prescribes some common behaviors and forbids other nonproductive, regressive behaviors in the organization.

Culture has also been seen as a pattern of shared basic assumptions that the group learns as it solves its problems of external adaptation and internal integration—ones that *worked well enough to be considered valid* and, therefore, are taught to new members as ways to perceive, think, and feel in relation to those problems.

The renowned culture expert Edgar H. Schein divides cultures into performing and nonperforming types. A performing culture is flexible and adaptable and promotes employee adaptation and relationships between members; it helps solidify all the golden principles of employee satisfaction and productivity.

Understanding your new world through the eyes of the people you are leading will help define your success. The present norms and values were not designed by you—you were not there when they were started or agreed upon as durable and acceptable. Your first job is to get to know these norms and values. Don't fool yourself—it is very important that you find out who you really are as well as strive for who you want to be. Doing a cultural assessment can provide you with measurable data about the real organizational values and norms that you need to know when planning for a new direction for the organization

I don't care what type of experience you are bringing into your new job, you can't be what you want to be or achieve want you want to achieve until you take time to study and master the new norms, values, and behaviors that have produced the present culture. Much of your work as a leader is about finding the right people who can help create the right culture—one that will help improve performance, productivity, and employee loyalty. Your new role is finding the right people with the right skills for the tasks and roles ahead of you as the organization's point guard. You need people who are ready to follow your new direction and new purpose, which will lead to the creation of a new working environment that promotes strong working relationships and a high-performing team.

You may be asking yourself the following questions: *Why do I have to do this? How will I do this?* These two questions are legitimate because of where you have been and what you have achieved as a health-care executive. The argument is not about what you have done or what you are going to do, rather it is about your organization's future. Yes, you are a seasoned CEO with years of experience and a record of accomplishments. Failure to devote your energy to this golden principle could derail you from your goals or vision for the organization. Your willingness to understand the new environment, culture, and values will not only be good for the organization but could also define your leadership and your ability to move the organization to the next level of development. Your goal is to move this new organization to the future and take it from good to great. The social structure of the organization must allow for a dual relationship between those in positions of authority and workers.

As a new CEO/leader, getting to know your people and learning about other areas of the organization, without compromising your position or prestige, will allow you to have good knowledge of the organization and bring about the necessary changes to the present culture. The right culture is not always easy to create. Your job is to let your team know that great organizations are those with a culture that is open to change. An organization with a performing culture is one that is ready for new tasks and challenges, ready to develop a new paradigm that is effective and easier to align with today's realities. The willingness and readiness to move away from the present comfort zone to an unseen territory will help you with your job and allow your shareholders to see the organization as one of the future. It must be communicated to the members of the organization that the only way to move on and begin to look to the future is through a readiness to change from the present culture or modify behaviors that have developed out of the present culture.

It must be understood that culture cannot be produced by individuals acting alone. Culture originates as individuals interact with one another—it is a byproduct of what members agree to be normal. Persons who do not endorse and practice prevailing beliefs, values, and norms become marginalized and may be punished or expelled from the society. The organization's norms must support or reflect the values of the organization, which automatically lead to or produce a socially accepted behavior. Deviant behaviors should be discouraged because of their negative influence on the overall goal of the organization.

Learning and adjusting to a new culture will require you to learn the three key levels that are associated with a culture: cultural artifacts, values, and shared tacit assumptions.

Cultural artifacts are what is most noticeable to your customers and employees as soon as they come into contact with your organization. These can be assessed by what they see, hear, and feel during this initial contact.

Values are beliefs that the people in the organization espouse. Some of these values may center on things like teamwork, open management style, employee empowerment, and a two-way communication style by the leaders. To understand this level, the new leader has to observe, explore, and ask questions pertaining to these espoused values.

The last but not the least of these levels is *shared tacit assumptions.* To be able to understand what this means to the organization a new leader must think historically about the organization and look at the values, beliefs, and assumptions of the founders and key leaders who made it successful.

The leader should understand that the work environment serves as a forum for different behaviors that are within the constructs of the norms of the organization. These organizational norms are groups of expected behaviors and ways of communicating that are defined and approved by interactions, experience, and organizational values.

The drive for a new culture must not be centered on internal advantages alone, but should also be stressed outside the organization. The leader must see the new culture as one that will shape the identity of the organization in the minds of customers.

What are your customers saying about your people, your services, and the interactions they experience when they are in your organization? It is very important for you to clarify how you want to be identified by your customers and then tries to make that real for both your customers and your employees. By redefining the culture from the outside—through customer's eyes—you are laying a foundation for commitment and loyalty that can help build and sustain a pool of happy and loyal employees. Leadership behaviors must be seen as effective and influential; therefore, it is important that you use the new culture to create new behavior patterns among your people. Creating a shared understanding of the key goals for the cultural change through the use of appropriate and influential leadership behaviors will mean a lot to all members of the organization.

There are two types of human behaviors—nourishing and toxic—and it is very important for you to encourage the kind that will help solidify and reinforce desired outcomes and behaviors. Nourishing behaviors cause others to feel valued, capable, loved, respected, and appreciated. Toxic behaviors, in contrast, cause others to feel devalued, inadequate, angry, frustrated, or guilty.

Your role is to discourage toxic behaviors by encouraging productive and pleasant behaviors among your leadership team. Nourishing behaviors exhibited by the leadership will help in the creation of the new culture. The influence of the leader directly affects employee behaviors and attitudes. Therefore, your goal is to make sure that your cultural behaviors and expectations are demonstrated by everyone on your team. Do not allow your employees to see your determination to create a new culture as being exclusive. Everybody must be included in order for a meaningful culture change to happen.

Questions to Ask Yourself
- How are health-care leaders prepared to deal with

changing demands on their organizations? What have you done personally to prepare yourself for these demands?

• Have you noticed any behaviors that you think can be improved or sustained by changing your organization's culture? What approaches are you going to use to bring about the cultural change and why do you think these approaches will help you create a culture of success?

• Keeping in mind that the pillar of a good culture is its people, how involved are your people in creating your new organization's culture?

Behavior #2:
Use Effective Communication

I have been in health care all my life, and I have often heard managers and leaders talk about why it is so important to communicate with staff. As a leader, you must know that your employees have the right to know where they fit into the organizational structure and understand the importance of what they have contributed to the success of the organization. As one CEO said to his leadership team, "There is no substitute for direct communication."

Effective communication is a critical tool for the effective and successful leader. Communication increases awareness of the organization's goal and mission; it helps promote loyalty, trust, and respect for the leader and his program; it helps remove resistance to change. There are many reasons why good communication is necessary. Organizations are departing from long-held beliefs and moving toward new forms of association, relationships, and thinking, which is a paradigm shift in how businesses and relationships are viewed by members of the organization. These new relationships and behaviors come at a unique stage in history. The new demands require organizations to construct a new reality based upon rational and universal principles and norms.

The presence of collective bargaining in organizations has been attributed to poor communication by the leaders. It is common to find leaders blaming themselves for inviting bargaining units into their organization because of poor communication. In retrospect, this assumption is right; but not all bargaining units in organizations are a result of poor communication. There is usually more than one factor that contributes to it.

The Christian faith understands the importance of communication to evangelism and how people respond to their preaching and teaching. We know that Christ, when commanding his disciples to go out in the world and spread the gospel, asked, "How can they know, if they have not been told?" He also asked how they could change "if they have not been preached to."

How can your employee do what needs to be done if he or she has not been told or communicated to regarding the new direction, the new structure, and the new expectations? Through communication, you can help create a strategic direction for the members of your organization. The strategic direction you are creating could develop into an empowered workforce that believes in and understands the organization's desire for a better future. Organizational studies have told us that leadership's ability to communicate the vision, the plan, and the strategy for future development is a determining factor for the success or failure of an organization. Good communication from an organization's leaders will ensure congruency among the workforce. This is important because communication remains the most valuable tool a leader has to enhance performance and employee satisfaction and loyalty.

To make your communication most effective, the following steps must be taken. The sender must be sure that the message is clear enough for the receiver to understand; it must also be timely and meaningful to both the sender and the receiver. The next stage is for the sender to make sure that the communication is delivered with respect and understanding of what the other party may be going through. This is a very important stage for any effective communication because it leads to the trust that is needed for the final outcome—which is the action taken in response to the message.

The chart below shows these communication-related steps:

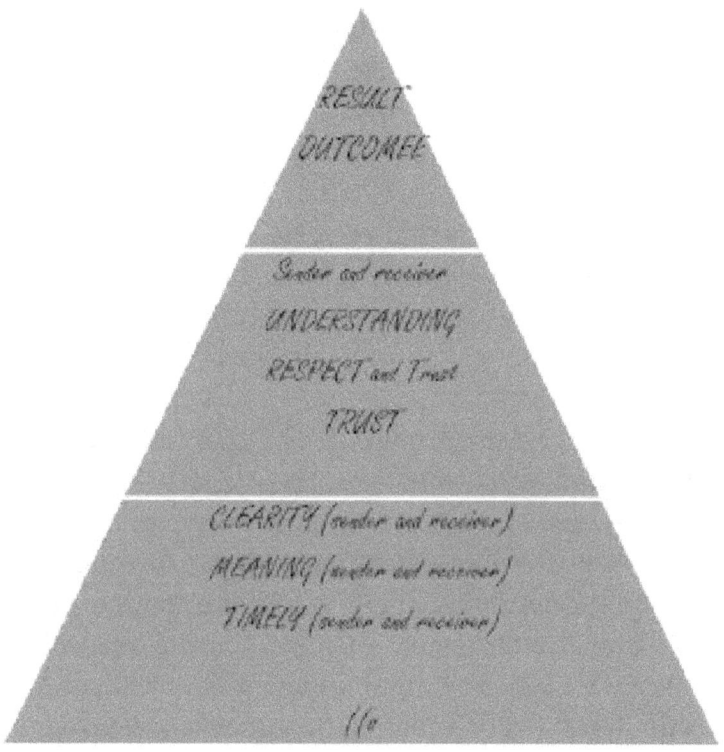

In his book *The Speed of Trust: The One Thing That Changes Everything*, Stephen Covey writes that for communication to be effective and trust to be established, it is very important for the leader to do the following:

- Disclose and reveal expectations clearly.
- Discuss and validate them for understanding.
- Never assume that expectations are clear or shared.

Finally, you must be sure that the commitment that you get is real and not fake. It must be a commitment that originates from total understanding of the *what* and the *why* of the message.

I remember when my organization was going through a tough financial period. We were putting people on standby, calling them off, and even putting some major projects that had been identified as key for the organization's growth on hold. People were using their saved time to make up for the hours they did not work. People were hearing different rumors every day—for instance, that the hospital had been sold, that the organization was going to lay off lots of people, and that the organization could no longer put money into the employee retirement fund and was instead taking money out of it to meet monthly payroll obligations.

The leaders in the organization got together and came up with a good communication technique. The president held multiple town hall meetings at which he explained to employees what was going on and answered questions pertaining to the rumors. Our communication during this period was excellent: people were informed as to how the organization was going to deal with each problem. Without good communication by the president and his leadership team, I don't think the organization could have overcome its problems the way it did.

Your own personal communication style is very important. Good communication is essential for you to be able to influence policy and behaviors within the organization. Your communication skills will define you as a leader. Communication is a lubricant for effective change. Because you play a very important role in the organization, it is necessary for you to identify your communication style and skills and the effects they have on the organization. We know from the literature written by experts that leadership communication style will remain an important tool that inspires employees to do more for the organization.

When you cannot communicate effectively with your staff, you create room for rumors, dissatisfaction, and a high stress level among your employees. Your lack of communication can also lead to the creation of informal leaders who are not necessarily in line with your viewpoint or your direction for the organization. Use your staff meetings to promote dialogue. I have seen meetings at which the only person who talks is the leader. When it gets to question-and-answer time, the room is as quiet as a graveyard. Nobody talks or contributes to the discussion. A failure to ask questions may be a sign of discomfort or fear among your staff. Find time to diagnose the problem—why are they not talking or contributing to the discussion? If you are a controller—someone who loves to lead, dominate, and be right at all times—you need to check your leadership style. This may be the reason why your followers are not comfortable during meetings and are not contributing meaningfully to the discussion.

As a director, I have received feedback of various kinds from my staff regarding my communication style. Some said I yelled when talking to them; others said they found it difficult to understand me or hear what I said. In solving these problems, I did a lot of self-assessment. When I went to my staff, I found that 90 to 95 percent of them said they had not observed me yell when talking to them; others said that when I talked to them on the phone, they found it very difficult to understand what I was trying to get across but when talking to them face to face, they clearly understood me. I now check myself when talking and use e-mail more frequently to send messages to staff. If I need an immediate response, I make sure I go to people's offices instead of calling them on the phone. Understanding and respect is very important for effective communication.

Your ongoing effort to educate, update, and motivate your staff through good communication will reinforce their commitment as well as their individual beliefs in shared governance, which produces better membership buy-in, performance, and attitude. Use your communication style to accomplish the following:

- Communicate expectations
- Communicate accepted behaviors
- Communicate your vision
- Communicate new developments within the organization
- Communicate the urgency around your goals
- Communicate your positions on issues that are important to your organization and employees
- Create a viable and caring work environment

As a leader, your ability to create urgency around your program through communication will help you move the organization to the next level. The new health-care environment needs leaders with a high level of interpersonal skills and the ability to communicate, motivate, and mobilize people toward common goals. Poor communication cannot produce good fruit. Literature has shown that good communication produces a safe and secure work environment and a positive, nurturing health-care environment.

Given your leadership style and how you communicate, what do you think your staff would say if asked to comment on the following issues?

1. How they feel when they talk to you
2. How easy it is to communicate with you or bring issues of interest to you
3. How well you listen to them when they are telling you about things that are bothering them
4. How easy it is to say what they are really thinking
5. How important is their contribution and how you use their contribution when planning for the strategic goals of the organization
6. Whether they think you understand them or try to

understand them
7. Whether they feel free to disagree with you on issues

Questions to Ask Yourself
- What is your personal communication style? How do you communicate your views to your fellow workers?
- What are five characteristics of effective communication style and what are five characteristics of ineffective communication style? Your response should be based on your experiences.

Behavior #3:
Be Visible

One factor that is essential to the creation of a performing organization is the level of engagement and involvement of the leadership in the day-to-day activities of the organization. A leader who is visible at all times creates a better working environment and lends a sense of support to employees. Your role as a leader is to help your frontline staff and other members of the organization to tailor their efforts to the overall goals of the organization. Through your presence, you are able to see, feel, and hear what your people are going through. You are also showing them that you are open to new knowledge, new thinking, and new approaches.

One advantage of a leader's visibility comes from his or her interactions with patients. I have heard leaders talk about their meetings with patients. Most of these talks are positive. Most patients consistently express a desire to be part of the decision making about their care. The presence of the CEO or the leader in their rooms speaks volume, as they are able to talk about their care, how they are been treated, and how they view their caregivers.

Another advantage of leadership visibility is that it promotes employee commitment. In *The Speed of Trust*, Stephen Covey states that the degree of commitment held by employees is based on the level of trust they have in their leader. He says that "the ability to establish, grow, extend, and restore trust with workers is the key leadership competency of the new global economy." Visibility helps you to build the trust you need to engage your team, your workers, and your organization. Letting them know they can see you when they want to and that they don't have to wait before their questions or concerns are answered lays the foundation for a long-lasting working relationship and trust. Without adequate understanding by your employees of your role and function in the organization, it will be difficult for them to believe you or take you seriously. It is unlikely that your followers will be able to talk about, advocate for, or defend your position and vision to your customers if they are not sure about it. It is very important that a leader be constantly in touch with the members of the organization, explaining his or her views on what is going on in the organization. Leadership visibility will help prepare followers for the new economy and new behaviors.

The following advantages have been attributed to leadership visibility in the organization:

1. Leaders learn more about the organization, including changes that are taking place in it.
2. Leaders learn more about the beliefs and behaviors of the members of the organization.
3. Leaders have opportunities to offer instant thanks and rewards for good behaviors by employees that promote the organization.
4. It is a mechanism for immediate service recovery by the leader.
5. It eliminates the notion of us against them.
6. It improves organizational communication.
7. It promotes trust and respect in the organization.
8. It helps create a caring work environment.
9. It is a good listening tool for the leader.

How can you make yourself more visible? As a new nurse, I could not tell the difference between my manager and my director because they were always on my floor at the same time talking or helping with patient-care problems. My manager was on the floor calling doctors for nurses, noting physician orders, and, at the same time, observing what was going on. The nursing director was on the floor making rounds and talking to patients, nurses, nursing assistants, and physicians. Her presence allowed her to know more about the unit and the staff and, above all, be able to feel for what was going on and make things better for every worker. During one of my yearly evaluations, I asked my manager why she and her boss (the director of nursing) were always on the floor. She replied by saying, "To be effective, a leader must be visible and approachable." The leader must get away from her office and begin to work around, talk to the staff, feel for what is going on, and take the temperature of the units. If you stay in your office all the time, you are perceived to be invisible by your workers; your ability to move or change the work culture will be difficult, if not impossible. As a leader, you should know how to use your visibility to create an engaged workforce.

One thing that I took with me when I left Washington Hospital Center in D.C. was the power of visibility. The then-president of the hospital, Mike, was visible and available to all employees. He made rounds and helped people in various departments. He used his visibility to ask questions of and answer questions from the employees. Because of his behavior and his visibility, other members of the executive team were also visible. My vice president of patient care services, Sandy, could be seen everywhere, talking and listening to nurses, writing down their concerns, and answering questions she could answer immediately. The effect this unique leadership behavior had on the rest of the management team was to increase the visibility of junior and mid-level managers. We increased our visibility on our respective floors. Through this single behavior, we were able to build respect that facilitated better understanding and commitment from our staff.

Physicians are strong partners for improving care delivery. They have no time to come see you in your office with their problems or concerns. Most of them don't like to waste time in the hospitals—they want to come in and leave quickly. The good news is that being around will allow you to see these physicians in hallways, parking lots, and physician lounges. It is also a good practice for you to go to their offices. Your visibility to physicians will improve your relationships with them. By making yourself available to physicians, you are telling them that you care, that you are ready to listen, and that you are willing to work with them to improve care delivery.

In their research, House and Dessler state that "a supportive leader is the leader who provides guidance to followers, treats them fairly, and recognizes their inputs as valuable." There is no leadership behavior that allows leaders to fulfill these roles better than visibility and presence on the floor or on the front line. Your visibility behavior can be a bridge between you and your employees, creating intimacy and attachment. When your employees know that they are not alone and have support for their actions, and can see from your behaviors that you care for them and their welfare, they will begin to develop a lasting working relationship with you, which will lead to better employee productivity and performance.

Questions to Ask Yourself
- What are the advantages of leadership visibility?
- What are the barriers to effective leadership visibility? How can a leader work around them?
- How should leaders use visibility to promote their agenda?
- How often do you leave your office to make rounds and talk to your employees?

Behavior #4:
Choose Your Words Carefully to Build Employee Pride and Association

Every idea and every word that comes out of your mouth is held to be true; therefore, use your words carefully. Use them for motivation, team building, and engagement. Your goal as a leader is to promote a peaceful and enjoyable work environment, a place where people feel valued and respected. Your words should help reinforce these two basic principles of respect among your followers.

Individuals experience a subjective reaction to words; therefore, leaders must be aware of what they say and how they communicate. It is very important for leaders to understand the power that is in their words. Leaders who start their daily briefings by energizing their audience through the use of encouraging words will have success in implementing their goals for the organization.

The work environment that you help create as a leader will determine your organization's performance and your employees' productivity. We know that every workplace promotes different behaviors and attitudes, and these have consequences for organizational behaviors and communications, as these behaviors are byproducts of the organization's culture, norms, and values, which define the organization to those outside of it.

When talking about words, we are talking about the effect of a leader's words on employees' pride of association. Your words have weight and influence on how people see the organization and behave within it. Let us look at the impact words have on feelings, behaviors, motivation, and performance. In his 2006 book, *The 360 Degree Leader: Developing Your influence from Anywhere in the Organization,* John C. Maxwell alludes to the fact that the power of words is immense and that well-chosen words can stop a fleeing army and transform defeat into victory and save an empire.

We all know that the period encompassing the last four months of 2008 and all of 2009 was a financially difficult one for most health-care organizations. During these agonizing months, communication became so important for the leaders in these organizations. In my organization, our CEO held series of town hall meetings, which he used to inform the staff as to what the organization was doing to meet the challenges posed by the financial problems. What was very interesting to most of us on the leadership team was the response that we got from our staff members after each meeting. They were so appreciative of the way they were kept in the loop, and most importantly, of the motivating words used by the CEO. The financial crisis brought different reactions from the staff. Some were worried about their pensions. Most were scared and apprehensive. Nevertheless, they felt encouraged by the positive words that came out of the CEO's month—words that were motivating, encouraging, and respectful of individual feelings and concerns. The words used during these town hall meetings were not negative or demoralizing; instead, they promoted understanding and focused on the commitment needed to achieve the organization's common goals. The organization was able to withstand the storm and came out nicely because of this. You need to be able to find a common ground of agreement and find words that will help you move everyone toward that common ground.

It is crucial for you as a leader to be sure that your words are not confrontational, buck-passing, or accusatory. Let your words help you build a collective ideology and feelings of identification and ownership that will eventually galvanize your staff and promote cooperation and commitment. You must realize that it is your style and the attitude you display in your own message that will determine the response and attitude of your staff to your message. If you start meetings with words that are negative and an attitude that is defeating, then you should expect the same reaction from your audience. Always let your words carry a positive outlook when you engage in dialogue with the staff.

This brings me to the next important thing that you must be sure is present in your communications with staff. Your words must be clear enough for everyone on your team to understand. Be sure that you are using words that say what you mean and can at the same time appeal to your staff members' emotions and sense of group association. Be careful of words with multiple meanings and interpretations—these types of words not only demoralize staff but also interject meanings that you did not intend. To be taken seriously by your staff, you must use words that are familiar, meaningful, and colorful and create memories and pictures in their minds. Specificity is another thing that your words must be able to provide. Let your words help you explain your intentions, your feelings, and your admiration for your staff. Avoid foul language—such words will not help you achieve your goal. Your bad words could spell doom for the organization; they could be seen by your staff as fostering an unsafe work environment.

One method that has been used to create reality by our staff is known as the *conventional method*. Conventional reality creation can occur in the form of education, information, and association. In creating a new reality, the leader must help people to create a new expectation around words. Staff members always attach meaning to what they think is true or perceive to be true. You must use your words positively if you want your staff to develop a new reality that will improve the culture and bring positive alignment between behavior and performance.

Every leader must understand that the knowledge of the world, self, and others is a byproduct of language, and language is a precondition for the act of becoming aware of oneself as a distinct entity. Words convey multiple meanings, and often people use words to signify things quite different from the words' original meanings. It is very important for you as a leader to make sure that your use of words is not conveying a meaning that is different from what you intend. When staff members perceive that their leader is truthful to his words and that he means what he says, they will not only be motivated to heed the words, they will also attribute certain positive leadership traits, such as trust and honesty, to the leader. The advantage will not only be seen in their interactions with the leaders but also in their attitudes, values, and behaviors, which will be consistent with what the leader wants.

Questions to Ask Yourself
- What are some encouraging words that you have used as a leader?
- Why do leaders use words that fail to represent their intentions or goals?
- Can you list ten motivating and encouraging words?
- Can you list ten words that you would not encourage a leader to use?

Behavior #5:
Develop a Culture of Safety

A safe culture is a wary culture, one that has a collective mindfulness of the things that can go wrong.
—The Joint Commission

The espoused values of an organization and the behavior, attitudes, and beliefs of its employees all give a perfect picture of how people see safety in the organization. The meaning and perception of safety by your customers reflect their observations and experiences of what and how they are treated when using your services. In developing a culture of safety, it is paramount that leaders get involved in the entire process. Your role as a leader is critical to the promotion of the perception of quality and a safe culture. We know through literature that leadership involvement has helped in the promotion of better care delivery in most health-care organizations.

The initial task for any health-care leader is to constantly demonstrate behaviors that are likely to promote and sustain a culture of safety. Your commitment to safety must be seen by your staff: you must speak it, walk it, and behave it. Your passion for safety should also be shown through your active participation in safety events, such as your investigating any incident that is not in alignment with the organization's position on safe behavior.

Another thing that you must advocate is risk taking, which can help you promote an adaptive work environment in which people are less afraid of dealing with critical issues they are facing. The culture must be nonpunitive and not intimidating to the staff. They should see their actions and behaviors on safety issues as those that are not going to jeopardize their jobs. We know that staff members are always willing to promote safety when they know that mistakes are not held against them—when they feel they can learn from their mistakes and take necessary actions that could help prevent future errors or mistakes.

Your process should be transparent and be used to emphasize the importance of personal responsibility and accountability. Your new culture must be a blame-free one that appreciates people and their efforts in making the organization error-free. The culture must foster a work environment that values continual learning based on individual voluntary disclosure of errors or problems around safety. As a leader, you need to know that creating a culture of safety must be a shared value between the leadership team and the staff.

Use your visibility to demonstrate your commitment to safety. Your physical presence in the facility could be used to assess and evaluate staff practices on safety and to talk about your dedication to safety culture. Putting safety first on the agenda at your staff meetings is another way of demonstrating your commitment to the issue. Let safety be the first thing you talk about and use every opportunity that you have to emphasize and promote it.

Another thing that is very helpful in creating a safety culture is having a safety officer. The role of this person is to help in the development of language and pictures that could help cement better safety behavior throughout the organization. The officer should report directly to the president and CEO of the hospital and should have a strong relationship with all health-care workers, including doctors, pharmacists, and nurses. It is this person's duty to talk to managers and the frontline staff when there is any safety problem.

When I was in Michigan; we hired a safety officer. The awareness that we saw throughout the organization was a result of this person's affinity for safety and his attitudes toward a just culture.

Your safety officer can be used to promote accountability. Employees always want to know what will happen to those who do not follow through on safety. Your staff must have confidence that everyone will be held accountable when it comes to safety. Sustainability of the new safety culture is possible only when there are consequences for behaviors that go against the general norms.

Another step could be having a safety focus group that includes your management team and frontline staff, both clinical and nonclinical. Let them help you define what the safety culture of the organization should be.

This group should have power and freedom on safety issues. The role of the group should be to help the organization address safety risks that impact people's behaviors and attitudes. Your leadership role is to make a visible commitment of time and money to this group. Your safety initiatives will be successful if you are able to get more people on your side; the broader the buy-in the greater the chances for success. This group needs motivation and inspiration from you in order to succeed. Your support will help them with their mission and objectives. Find means of providing timely feedback to them and be ready at all times to be their teacher and coach when they are facing difficult safety issues.

Having frontline staff at the table when you are designing your safety initiatives is critical to the organization's success. If they are able to identify, develop, and implement safety solutions they think will prevent mistakes, they are likely to be more committed to the plan than if they are just asked to help with implementation. Employee involvement enhances behaviors that are necessary for an organizational cultural change that will help foster an environment of safety, one that makes both employee and patient safety a priority.

You might want to borrow some ideas from retail companies in the realm of promoting safety. An example is the Wal-Mart organization. I was in one of their stores one day buying something for my daughter. I was paying for my purchases when I heard an announcement over the P.A. system asking all employees not attending to customers to take a moment to carry out a safety check. The announcement caught my attention. I left the cashier to go and see what type of behavior would be displayed by the employees. I was surprised to see employees looking around for things that might pose safety problems. If anyone were to find a safety problem, his or her role was to look for a solution to correct the problem.

Another company that has put more emphasis on safety is United Airlines. Michael Quiello, the airline's top safety officer, said this about safety and why it is very important for the company to pay more attention to it: "Whether in the air or on the ground, our number one priority is keeping our people safe. It is the foundation of everything we do at United Airlines." He further went on to say, "Safety is truly the responsibility of every employee at United—from our customer service representatives to our flight crews—and we expend considerable resources to provide the support, tools, and training our people need to create the safest possible work environment."

This sort of practice is what you need in your department or organization; your people must be able to set aside time out of their busy day to help you identify and correct any safety problems or concerns that they see in their respective departments or units.

When we are looking at developing a culture of safety, the commitment from the executive team provides a framework that is needed for the initial kickoff. Our leadership team expressed support with their behavior, attitude, and communication. The message was communicated via e-mails, at staff meetings, and by putting safety at the top of every leadership meeting's agenda.

Training is another component of a successful safety program. An organization that is striving to improve safety should emphasize staff training and development. Making training available to all employees indirectly shows a leadership commitment to a just culture. Your training program should not depend on the financial status of the organization; it should be seen as a necessity for the advancement of patient-care delivery and safety in the organization.

When my organization embarked on its journey of creating a culture of safety, we did not anticipate the financial crisis that hit us. We did all the planning and designing and engaged more staff in the initial phase of training. Unfortunately for us, the crisis happened and our financial position became questionable. There were a lot of discussions on whether the organization should continue with the staff training or not. We also looked at using a "train the trainer" methodology in order to save money and continue to show our staff the organization's commitment to the program. After thorough deliberation, the leadership decided to move on with the training. The training workshops were mandatory for all staff. We also provided some open training sessions to our physicians.

Some key lessons taught to the staff in this safety training related to safety behavior skills. We instructed our staff on how to use these skills when taking care of patients. I recommend that you find behaviors your employees will engage in that are helpful and meaningful for your safety initiatives.

Two particular skills are quite powerful if done right and can foster a culture of safety. These are questioning and verifying behaviors respectively. If every member on your team learns to take a few seconds to reassess his or her thoughts before acting on them, this process can help prevent unsafe practices that may be damaging to the organization.

The support that our leadership gave to the safety training program led to its successful implementation and increased awareness of safety issues among our staff. Because of our appreciation of the role of the frontline staff in the creation of a safety culture, and their knowledge of faulty systems, processes, and conditions within the organization, most of our instructors for safety training were frontline staff. This single act alone contributed to how well our staff embraced the initiative throughout the organization.

Collaboration among various departments within the organization is also essential for creating a culture-of-safety program, and leaders must encourage it so that the organization reaps the advantages. Your safety team or focus group must include every department within the organization. Each department has different safety issues. Having them share their different problem-solving skills can promote understanding between departments. For a successful culture of safety, the leader must focus not only on individual actions but also on how each department deals with transparency and behaviors that support the culture of safety. Through interdisciplinary collaboration, leaders should be able to assess those safety problems associated with a system failure. Those systemic factors must be looked into collectively for collaborative solutions. For this to be successful, leadership involvement is needed. A successful culture of safety depends on the quality of leadership provided to the team. The leader can use this interdisciplinary group to engage the staff in the safety initiative. Your interdisciplinary group should help build strong employee engagement and participation in safety. During your interaction with this group, seek input on issues that affect staff members and encourage them to implement their solutions for improving safety without fear of intimidation or punishment.

A true culture of safety is possible when there is true leadership and an organizational commitment to safety. Your timely intervention on safety issues brought to you will be crucial at the initial stage of the implementation. Staff members must see your stamp in all areas of the safety behaviors skills that are implemented.

The letters in the words *time* and *stamp* have special meaning for safety.

TIME Safety Behavior Skills for Frontline Employees

T= Think   Before embarking on anything, take a few moments to think.

I= Inspect   Use two to three seconds to inspect all of your steps. Are they appropriate?

M= Modify   Correct yourself or the action if you think there is a reason for modification.

E= Execute   When you are sure that all stones have been turned and all steps have been verified as correct, go on and execute.

STAMP Safety Behavior Skills for Leaders

S=Stop   It is very important for both the leader and the staff to take time to stop and regroup when it comes to safety.

T= Take   Everyone must know how to take a deep breath when feeling deeply stressed or overwhelmed. Breath

A=Assess   The group must assess and reassess the program, the steps, and actions already put in place.

M= Modify   If there is doubt, the team should find ways to adjust those areas that require modification.

P= Perform   After the assessment and modification have been done and are confirmed to be okay, then the team can go on and perform the acts or approve the actions.

The leadership's openness and its desire to communicate and demonstrate the importance of a safe culture to the survival of the organization will go a long way toward inculcating safe behaviors and a culture that values learning, reporting, and equal justice among employees.

Questions to Ask Yourself
- What actions have you implemented in your organization that have helped promote a culture of safety?
- What are some of the barriers to a just culture and what advice do you have for leaders facing these barriers?
- Do you think health-care organizations can be zero-error organizations? Why or why not?
- How do you receive information that is related to safety issues in your organization?

Behavior #6:
Focus on Staff Satisfaction to Build Customer Satisfaction

Your organization's success depends on two things: happy and satisfied employees and happy and loyal customers. Don't forget that there can be no happy and loyal customers if there are no happy and satisfied employees.

Caring for your most needed resources must be your primary objective if you want to see your organization move forward and compete with other organizations. Your customers assess your organization through what they observe in your employees' attitudes and interactions. How your employees communicate with and show respect to customers will define your organization for them. An organization improves if every employee is involved in the act of caring—for themselves, for the patients and their relatives, for the community as a whole.

Employee satisfaction is a byproduct of the perceptions, feelings, and interactions among people. As leader, you must understand that employees need to be able to express how they feel in the organization; therefore, the environment must be right and good for a mutual relationship.

There are six behaviors that have been accepted by successful leaders and managers as crucial to employee satisfaction. Such leaders and managers take time to listen to their employees, get involved in daily operations of the organization, and value diversity in its totality by understanding that there is more to be gained from a diverse group than from a nondiverse group. These leaders believe that to move an organization to the next level, they need to earn their employees' trust. Trust is essential to an organization's productivity.

The six behaviors are the following:
- Listening
- Communicating
- Trusting
- Supporting
- Rewarding
- Empowering

These six behaviors help create sense of purpose and ownership for the employee. Let us look at some of these six values to see how important they are to employee satisfaction and organizational performance.

Listen

If you ask successful leaders what has contributed to their success, I am very sure that many of them will answer that it was their ability to listen to people's concerns and feelings. To be willing and able to listen is the most needed skill of a leader. If you don't know how to listen, you will not know how to develop, maintain, and encourage participation and collaboration. Listening is the ability to hear with thoughtful attention what people say to you. If you want free, independent, and happy employees and customers, you need to know how to listen to what they say. Listening is about respect for feelings and concerns. Your role is to figure out how to deal with these.

When staff members come to me for solutions, I try to go into a proactive mode, not a reactive mode. The proactive mode helps me to reason with people based on what they are saying and what they want to hear about how to address an issue. I am able to reflect on what they are saying, which is what they want me to do when they talk to me. The reactive mode makes you miss important points that people are making, and it causes people to think that you are not approachable. When you take time to listen, you express your support for employees, which they need in order to cope with job stress. It also increases their sense of control, which has a direct effect on how they feel.

When we first began to talk about employee satisfaction and how we could help enhance loyalty and improve productivity, we developed a group of managers and staff called the senior rounding group. The purpose of this group was to make daily rounds with our staff and visit patients having problems with their care. This group was so effective that we saw both patient and employee satisfaction increase. Our employees were happy because they knew that whenever they raised an issue of concern to any member of the senior rounding group, it would be looked into with limited delay. The same was true for our customers: they knew that our people were there to listen to whatever problems they might have had.

It is important to demonstrate to your customers and employees that their feedback is needed and meaningful for organizational development. Listening is a practice that you can use to reward and acknowledge your people's efforts and performance. You will also discover things that demand your immediate attention when you listen.

Listening to your customers is also important. The following are some of the advantages your organization will enjoy due to your willingness to listen to customers' problems.

- It shows that the organization genuinely cares about their well-being.
- It shows that the organization is willing to help solve problems.
- It shows that the organization is able to help customers and takes time to hear their concerns.
- It shows that the organization tries to understand customers' needs.

- It creates the perception that the organization is capable of listening to the voices of its customers.

The following tools can help you be a good listener in your organization:
- Focus groups
- Customer surveys
- Personal conversations
- E-mails
- A newsletter
- Employee feedback on customer needs and wants

Communicate

As you begin your journey toward creating a better organization in which freedom, happiness, and creativity are experienced by every member, you need to believe in the power of communication. As described in the previous chapter, communication is the lubricant for moving an organization forward. Your people are not going to be motivated or energized if they don't know what you stand for, where you are going, and what you are demanding from them. It is clear communication that helps explain the vision and mission of the organization. Literature has shown that communication between leaders and employees has a big impact on organizational loyalty.

As a leader, I hold dearly to this theory on communication in how I manage my staff. As a foreign-born person, I have been told that it is often difficult to understand what I say, especially over the telephone. Because of this, I use various methods of communication, but the one that I enjoy most is face-to-face communication.

Make sure your behavior is consistent with what you say. In other words, let your communication themes be seen in your behavior. When your behavior is perceived to conflict with what you are communicating, there will be a tendency for disconnection and dissatisfaction on the part of employees. When your employees are not sure they can dialogue with you due to their fear of been punished or reprimanded, you create an environment that is not supportive or encouraging creativity. When you take creativity away from your staff, you are promoting status-quo employees, submissiveness, and less-empowered employees.

Let your communication be meaningful, specific, and clear to your employees. I have found myself in various kinds of trouble because of failure to do this. I was involved in a conflict that changed my view about people and how dysfunctional we can be. It happened when my hospital was thinking of making a huge structural change in our management. The organization decided to put me in charge of three additional units beyond those I was already heading. Before the transition, I met with some of the leaders of these units and let them know how I wanted them to operate. I told them I was in favor of fewer meetings and that; therefore, we would be meeting a half hour before our meeting with the hospital vice president patient-care services. I was shocked when told by our human resources manager that these people came to her and said, "The half hour meeting is to be used to find out what they have in mind or on the agenda for our meeting with the VP." I was dumbfounded and speechless because that was not what I had said when I had met with them.

It is very important for you to explain in clear terms what you mean and what you want people to do. It is also a good practice to ask for feedback on what you have said.

It is important to keep your people informed about things that are going on in the organization. When they are informed, they will be able to help you look for new customers and retain staff. This also fosters a peaceful working environment. Keeping employees informed and up-to date contributes to the level of trust and loyalty the employees have for the organization.

Ongoing communication helps build a meaningful and respectful working relationship between you and your staff. Use your communication to ask questions on how you can help make employees' jobs easier and achievement of their goals less painful.

I recollect a conversation I had with one of my managers sometime in 2009. We were doing massive staff education on new behavioral standards, and I was one of the major trainers. During the year, we discovered that a particular unit did not have enough employees in this training; therefore, we had to come up with a plan for getting most if not all trained by a deadline. During my conversation with the manager of this unit, she told me she had arranged for another trainer to come and train her staff. My response to her was to ask why we could not register her staff with those classes that I would be teaching, as these classes had employees from other departments as well, and, most important, I did not know whether these classes were full. I instructed her to talk to my assistant and let her help with this registration. She expressed her thanks and called the other instructor from our sister hospital to tell her of our new plan. Weeks later, I was surprised to hear that this manager had told the human resources manager that I had "forced her to cancel her original plan."

What I want you to get from this incident is that this manager did not show any dissatisfaction with this decision that we jointly made. The training went well, and she even gave me good feedback. We were able to train 85 percent of her staff.

It is very important for you as a leader to conclude your discussions by asking questions. Ask your staff members if the decision you have made is okay with them. Ask about any concerns before you wind up the

conversation. Be on the lookout for any misinterpretations, as your staff can use this against you.

Trust

When we talk about trust, we always think of honesty and purity. Trust is the totality of what makes a good and effective leader. Trust is the foundation for employee satisfaction and happiness. Trust is the key to good customer recruitment for the organization; it brings people to the organization because they know what they will get from it is real and sincere. Customers are looking for an organization that is trustworthy—one they can believe in.

According to Kane-Urrabazo (2006), trustworthiness is a result of character and competence; it is what you gain when people believe in you and have confidence in you. Trust is a value that should be held by all members of the organization including the leadership team. Each department leader or manager should know that trust is a crucial element that links employee performance, customer loyalty, and organizational commitment.

What should be done to sustain behaviors that help promote culture that is built on trust and commitment? I will share with you what Stephen Covey wrote in *The Speed of Trust: The One Thing That Changes Everything*. He listed the following behaviors that are seen in a high-trust organizations.

- Information is shared openly.
- Mistakes are tolerated and encouraged as a way of learning.
- The culture is innovative and creative.
- People talk straight and confront real issues.
- Transparency is a practiced value.
- People are candid and authentic.
- There is a high degree of accountability.
- There is real communication and real collaboration.

To run a productive organization, you need to make sure that all these behaviors are mandatory for everybody. Preach these behaviors every day and encourage your employees to demonstrate them when dealing with each other and with customers.

Support

Whenever I go for an interview, I ask my future leader what type of support I can expect to receive from him or her. To be successful, I need the support of my leader. I like to know if he or she will be there for me when the waves come. There is nothing as disheartening and frustrating for employees as feeling they don't have the support of their manager or leader.

When we were going through our magnet journey at Sparrow Hospital, my staff knew that they had my support with any decisions that came out from the unit-based council meetings. My support was crucial if I really wanted a functioning unit-based council. As a registered staff nurse in those days, I used to hear from my colleagues how happy they were to be working for our manager. When you asked them why, most of them would say resoundingly and overwhelmingly that it was because she was caring and supportive. They said she went all the way to find answers to their problems and supported them when the situation looked bleak and unsolvable.

On the other hand, I have heard from some colleagues that they left their units or managers because they did not view the person as a supportive leader, this person was not on their side, this person always supported the opposing party and disrespected them in order to make the other side feel happy with their decision.

Your support as a leader will help with retention, satisfaction, and loyalty. Your support will help you create that trusting relationship that is so important for your leadership ability and achievement.

Reward

I know that we all know the role rewards and recognition play in staff morale and productivity. My advice to you is to take time to look at your rewards program and come up with any modifications that are needed. I can tell you that many organizations continue to struggle with this concept.

You need to identify what works for your organization. Some leaders prefer a direct reward system, while others encourage an indirect method. A direct reward is given as soon as the good behavior occurs—it is immediate. There are also *local* and *network* rewards. Both local and direct rewards speak to the same concept. A local reward is a token of appreciation within a department, whereas a network reward is an organizational reward. A manager who encourages employee appreciation within her unit is promoting a local and direct reward system. On the other hand, any organization that ensures that performance by its members is recognized either at a leadership meeting or at a leadership forum is promoting what is known as indirect, or network, appreciation.

Another thing to have in mind is how each professional culture sees rewards. From my practice, I observed that clinical nurses prefer direct local rewards and recognition by their immediate supervisors, while physicians like organizational rewards from the company's CEO. When I noticed that one of my nurses had done something above what was expected, I made sure this nurse was rewarded openly at the nurse's stations, thanked him or her for a job well done, and read out loud to the rest of the staff any letters from customers that expressed appreciation for his or her care and compassion. This kind of reward helps with motivation and promotes satisfaction.

Empowerment

There is no leader who is going to say he or she does not know what employee empowerment means to the organization. We know through literature that empowerment is an important driver of organizational effectiveness and performance. Empowerment is the single biggest factor that motivates and energizes workers to go beyond expectations. We also know that empowering leadership might influence the overall performance of the organization by encouraging knowledge-sharing and participation.

When your organization is perceived as an empowering organization, a place where decision-making authority is delegated, allowing the employee to analyze, develop, contribute, and perform their duties without fear of failure, the probability that employees will help or influence decision making within the organization is higher. Empowerment helps remove the idea of micromanagement from the minds of the workers. When people are encouraged to take part in decision making, they will be actively engaged in the process of quality improvement by fully utilizing the resources at their disposal. The more group members participate in group decisions, the more resources are available that can positively affect the organization's performance.

Empowerment also helps increase employees' commitment and buy-in attitude yielding better organizational allegiance. That is the reason why I like the Baptist health principle of "no secrets and no excuses." Everything must be open and available with no red tape. All available data on quality, satisfaction, and performance must be shared with employees. This is how they are able to contribute meaningfully to the debate on the organization's future. Your employees must know where they stand in the organization and how much they have contributed to overall goals and objectives. Your employee empowerment program can help you change your people's behavior, level of satisfaction, and perception of leadership.

A well-developed empowerment program will help improve all of the following:
- Knowledge-sharing among members
- Member performance
- Organizational performance
- Employee satisfaction
- Employee participation
- The relationship between leaders and followers
- Employee readiness

Employee feelings of empowerment will also have a direct impact on how members feel about their sense of belonging at work. On the positive side, we have seen organizations that have used empowerment to increase support and influence, which has been found to directly correlate with recruitment and retention of highly skilled workers. Support should be one of the methods used by the organization in building power into the people. The key to having happy employees in your organization is letting go of power and creating more chances for the growth of staff members, both personally and professionally.

I have seen organizations that have recognized the importance of both employees and customers to what they do. They believe getting to the top requires partnerships between the organization, customers, leaders, and employees. They believe that a focus on customers means an increase in operational efficiency and product quality.

One of these organizations is the Baptist health-care system. In his book *The Baptist Health Care Journey to Excellence: Creating a Culture That Wows,* Al Stubblefield discusses why the system continues to maintain its top standing in both patient and employee satisfaction. "We can't hope to fulfill our vision of being the best health-care provider in the nation without hiring and retaining an excellent workforce. Until every employee is sold on and engaged in what we are trying to do, we will never be able to deliver consistent world-class service to our customers."

When defining a learning organization, Peter Senge wrote that a learning organization is one that fosters employee growth and development, a place where risk and learning are allowed to happen simultaneously. Learning organizations operate according to certain mental models related to the attitudes of the organization's members toward themselves and others and toward learning and the type of relationship that exists among employees, the community, and the shareholders.

Questions to Ask Yourself
- How does customer satisfaction help you with your overall objectives?
- What efforts have been made by your organization to improve satisfaction?
- What are four major things your organization could improve that would have lasting effects on your customers and their perceptions of your services?

Behavior #7:
Set Expectations

A performance-oriented culture is one in which every member of the organization understands what is expected of him and also understands the need to create unity of purpose to enhance outcomes.

You need to be able to create for your people a set of expectations that you think could carry you to your final destination. These expectations are the key ingredients for better employee engagement and performance. Employee participation should not be optional; everyone should be part of the journey and have something to contribute to the final outcome.

Expectations should be developed around organizational goals and objectives. What are the behaviors and attitudes that must be espoused by members of the organization that could be manifested in good outcomes and performance? As leader and manager, you should set expectations that are reasonable, achievable, and likely to have a positive effect on organizational identity, satisfaction, and the appreciation of human value. Anything contrary to these will not be good for the organization.

There are five types of expectations we need to address, as shown in the chart on page 50.

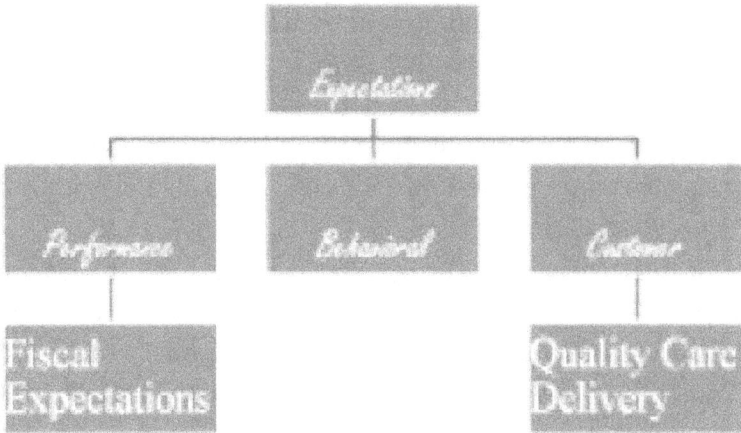

This chart, which I designed a long time ago, has helped me set expectations for my staff. The breakdown of these expectations is as follows:

Performance Expectations: For our department to meet our goals on patient care, each one of us will do our best to promote quality care, prevent errors by promoting safety, understand the complexity in human behavior, and look at our customers—our patients—holistically. We will take our time to find out and act on what is right the first time.

Behavioral Expectations: For our department to meet our goals on retention and loyalty, it is expected that we will respect each other, listen to each other, and communicate clearly with each other. We will honor our professional obligations through our behaviors and attitudes toward ourselves, our patients, and our coworkers. We will have trust in others and in what they do, be nonjudgmental, verbalize our concerns in a respectful manner, and finally, seek compromise when there is a conflict in ideas or perceptions.

Customer Service Expectations: In pursuit of our dream of being a great place to work, to provide good care, and to be a good partner to other caregivers, we will try to establish strong customer relationships with a new understanding of customer service and a strong commitment to deliver the best at all times. We will try to understand our customers, patients, and each other emotionally and spiritually. We will do everything to meet and exceed our customers' needs when interacting with them or carrying out our professional duties. We will not forget our patient-advocate role.

Fiscal Expectations: It is expected that we manage our resources well, use what we need, maintain a disciplined workforce around fiscal accountability, hold each other accountable, always press the green button after each trip to the supply machine, provide feedback to each other, report to work on time, respect shift-to-shift hand-off time, and help coworkers when they need help. We will not engage in any social activities that may delay or prolong shift reports. We will comply with all regulatory requirements on billing and charging.

Quality Care-Delivery Expectations: It is expected that all staff work toward this noble goal by making sure that the care delivered to customers is of high quality. We challenge each other with the "mother test." If your mother came to our department for care, could you rightly say that the care was good enough for her? Are you sure that you and your coworkers are able to deliver the type of care that you would want your mother to have?

How can these expectations be communicated to employees? The expectations you set will help you with role identification. People will know what these roles are and how to fulfill them when they are made aware of expectations. Clear guidance from you as the leader helps keep your staff on track and reduces the odds of their becoming fatigued and disengaged.

Participation and privileges should be communicated and should not be made optional for the staff. Let them know how they can best contribute to the achievement of goals. It is not acceptable to have people working for you who do not take part in any activities of the unit or the organization as a whole.

After each new employee orientation, I take time to go over my expectations and those of the department and the organization. I let the person know that we need a team player and that he or she is expected to work hard to be part of the team. These expectations are presented after the person is finished with hospital orientation and is in the unit.

I follow up every second mouth to make sure that these expectations are being met by any new staff members. The current staff members hold each other accountable and correct each other when there is a breach.

I often hear how it's getting difficult for leaders to hold people accountable for their actions. When I ask them why and what they are doing to correct this, the answer that I get is discouraging. I often hear things like "He is doing his job, and I don't want to offend him"; "He is my best worker"; "The rules and policies have made this impossible"; "It is too late to correct her"; "He belongs to a powerful group within the organization; therefore, it is difficult to correct him."

All of these excuses are possible because you have not sat down with your employees and gone over your expectations. Before it is too late, find time to write up your expectations in collaboration with your staff and present them to all your new hires as well as to the people presently working for you. You must know that some of these expectations will be uncomfortable and painful to some but pleasurable to others. You need to realize that these reactions from the group are temporary. Your support during this period of growing pains is very important for making your expectations the foundation for your culture.

Leaders who follow through on their expectations and demand accountability and responsibility help to create a better, more productive workforce and foster better care delivery. You must remember that you are leading two different categories of people: those who are ready and energized to go in the direction the organization is heading and those who are skeptical and always ask what the organization will do for them instead of what they will do for the organization. These groups need to understand what expectations you have of them in their roles and what you want them to contribute to the overall objective. It is not enough to just communicate expectations and direction; it is your responsibility to pay attention to what is going on in the organization

The expectations that you set must align with your organization's values. For you to turn commitment into strong performance, the personality and soul of the organization must be complemented by a set of expectations and behaviors that will motivate members of the organization to excel in what they do for the organization and for customers on a daily basis. It is this type of behavioral expectation that will help promote loyalty, which eventually leads to the productivity and satisfaction of your key resource—people.

Questions to Ask Yourself
- What are your expectations on performance, and how are you holding people accountable?
- What are the steps you will take to set and communicate your expectations on organization vision, mission, and values?
- Why do you think you need to set expectations when your objectives and goals are on track?

Behavior #8:
Promote Shared Governance

Leaders will have a vision, a passion, and an exciting aspiration. And this aspiration, once shared by everybody in the organization, will unleash tremendous human energy. —Rowan Gibson

Your goal should be to improve the quality-of-care delivery in your organization; therefore, your main objective should be centered on how to improve care continuity and relationships among the care providers and their leaders. A successful organization is one that believes in the collective skills of its workers. Shared governance is a practice that helps integrate all available skills in your organization. It is a practice that stands on one principle: the professional contributions from all its players.

According to the well-known writer and apostle of shared governance Porter-O'Grady, the following are some of the things shared governance within an organization can do:

- Increase participation in decision-making
- Develop collaborative relationships leading to the realization of team goals
- Make staff feel valued, leading to greater commitment and higher morale
- Ensure appropriate implementation and evaluation of ideas at the ward level
- Improve the quality of nursing care
- I personally think that through shared governance, additional good outcomes could be achieved, such as the following:
- Better employee morale

- Good and sustainable job satisfaction
- Good working relationships
- Improved staff loyalty and contributions to the organization
- Increased ownership, creativity, and identification• Better organizational performance and productivity.

Why do I think the solution to workplace problems is shared governance? I am saying this because I have seen positive results in organizations that have embraced this concept. When I came to my current job, the atmosphere was filled with negativity and low employee morale. This was seen all over the place—every department was experiencing some type of demoralizing leadership behavior. The hospital was also in the initial stage of putting people together for their magnet-recognition journey. This was not successful because of some opinions that employees had about the leaders and some managers.

We started a new approach that involved shared governance principles. We brought together employees from different departments; they were involved in decision making and came up with some recognition initiatives. At the end of the first fourteen months, we started noticing some improvements in morale and employees' sense of belonging. We also saw an increase in employee participation, morale, and satisfaction.

Shared governance contributes to better relationships between leaders and workers, which helps with the professional growth of the workforce. Shared governance is a two-tiered relationship-building structure that requires cooperation, trust, and excitement from both leaders and workers. There can be no shared governance when the above factors are missing.

How can you promote shared governance in your organization? You will need a new structure that supports shared leadership and shared governance. The new structure must recognize the power of a multidisciplinary team and the benefits inherent in power sharing. Shared governance, if implemented correctly, should foster a performing culture that believes in better participation and empowerment and develops all the professionals who work within the culture.

If your goal is to move your organization to the next level, an all-wheel drive, you need to find ways of including people in the decisions that directly affect their work and the organization's overall objectives. The new health-care organization can be possible only through a radical change in the relationships between leaders and followers. There must be a paradigm shift in how we see the role of employees in the realization of the organization's objectives.

The health care of the future will require cooperation and understanding between managers and workers within organizations. This new organization must continue to look for ways of building a trusting relationship that is based on mutual respect and understanding. Realistically, we know that increasing competition and intensity, reducing cycle time and costs, improving productive services, and meeting increasing patient demands are the key factors driving all organizations to change and define better working conditions for workers. These pressures require management to redefine and redesign how to act, think, and lead the operations. These situations demand managers to spend time figuring out what to do and how best to do it. The new solutions must be ones that add value to the overall objective of the corporation. Leaders must be careful not to overestimate their problem-solving skills, as the new work order will require that these skills be excellent.

Your full leadership support will be needed to institute shared governance. The future of the organization is not going to depend on the old tools—you will need new tools. You will need to adopt a management style that is far different from the traditional hierarchical, centrally controlled one. This new management style must be open, democratic, and willing to encourage creativity, critical thinking, and ingenuity. The workers must be able to challenge the status quo, take risks, and learn from their mistakes by finding solutions through teamwork. The environment must be friendly enough for open dialogue and expression of opinions on controversial topics. This type of leadership understands the power of collective bargaining. The new leadership style has to see the distribution of strategy making responsibility as the key for success, because shared governance is about responsibility, accountability, and ownership.

Shared governance needs a leader who has the wisdom, talent, and insight to motivate, encourage, and energize people to go in the right direction and who is able to create an environment where everyone can operate effectively. We have seen shared governance principles used to advance nursing practice, promote quality of care, and develop nursing strategy and employee loyalty in various magnet-recognized hospitals throughout United States.

The new health-care organizations are looking for leaders who see their position as a way to release the brain power of the organization and to generate intellectual capital. How can employees help you transform your organization when they are not consulted or given the power they need to implement the transformation?

I was impressed by a television interview I saw many years ago on the influence of a good, caring leader on his fellow workers. A gentleman who had begun his life with no hope and no vision for the future was living on the street and engaging in all types of unfulfilling activities. In his journey, he came across someone, a leader, who took him under his wing and nurtured him by caring for him and helping him set realistic goals and objectives. This man experienced a 180-degree turnaround in his life—he became a successful man with a bright future. When he was asked what made the difference, he said it was the leader who told him he cared about him and believed in him. This shows the power of leadership behavior on followers. Through well-defined and well-developed shared governance principles, your organization can also see a turnaround in employee behavior, performance, and loyalty.

The way jobs are designed has an effect on employee performance. Jobs designed to enrich the work climate by providing autonomy, responsibility, and the ability to complete work has a positive impact on the work group. If we as managers have positive effects on work groups, the workers will be more satisfied and confident.

If we think our current workers are too demanding, we have not seen anything yet. The new workers entering our organizations today are even more so. This new population will require us to rethink our views on behaviors, skills, communication, relationships, and decision making. This population has been fed and equipped by the new information technology. To lead them successfully, leaders and managers have to provide a new social apparatus in terms of relationship building and work performance.

You will see massive changes taking place in response to these behavioral changes and the needs of this new set of workers. For example, what happens to your retention, recruitment, and staff-development programs will reflect the overall view and behaviors of leaders in the industry on how they are working with this new population.

In an industry in which all organizations provide the same services, the only thing that will help separate your organization from the rest is the perception of the organization by those who work for it. The work environment should be one that is seen as a place where people want to work, one that reflects their values and lifestyles, one where they can realize their own growth and development.

All of us strive to be learning organizations, but this is possible only when our workers feel that their environment reflects what they actually value and experience daily. One thing that I know to be true is that the quality of employees' relationships with leaders has a significant effect on the productivity and happiness of the workers.

You might be asking yourself why you need to change or you may be thinking that your organization has had many productive years because of the relationships and working conditions that you have created. I am not saying this is not true; what I am saying is exactly the opposite—that the more specialized and bigger you have become as an organization, the more need there is for good behaviors related to relationships, communication, and decision making if you want to be successful as an organization.

As your organization expands its services and workforce, you will have to narrow your focus on what you can do to retain your best workers and, more important, on how you will attract new skilled and resourceful workers into your organization.

The old traditional concepts no longer work as well today. They have reached the end of the road. It will be advantageous for the organization to have leaders that believe in and are passionate about the new management concept of shared governance. As you are thinking about this concept, you must also know that shared governance is not a quick fix for organizational problems; it must be understood that involvement of all staff requires time, persistence, determination, and strong commitment to training and development.

Studies show that nine out of ten people say they like to be among positive people. This shows that if you can work on how to make your work environment more positive and friendly, you can move your organization to the next level.

Questions to Ask Yourself
- How are you going to support the practice of shared governance in your organization?
- What do you see as the possible barriers to the implementation of shared governance and how are you going to remove them?
- How can you sell the idea of shared governance in a more traditional organization, where it will not be an easy sell?
- What five strategies do you think will make shared governance planning, designing, and implementation go smoothly for your organization?

Behavior #9:
Be a Quality Leader

Organizations that demonstrate an understanding of the relationship between quality and performance are true organizations because of their devotion to continuous improvement.

There can be no improvement in the area of quality when leadership presence is missing. Research on this subject has shown time and time again that there is a direct relationship between the role of a leader and quality improvement. Hiscock and Shuldham (2008) point out in their article "Patient-Centered Leadership in Practice" that good leadership is important in setting the direction of an organization, developing its culture, ensuring delivery of services, and maintaining effective governance. You, the leader, must help the organization set strategic goals for quality improvement.

There can be no serious quality program in any organization without solid and reputable leadership support. For any quality-improvement program to be successful, leadership must be transformational and willing to change current practices through evidence-based initiatives. Furthermore, there must be a quality department in the organization, and it must be led by a well-qualified improvement specialist who can provide a link between the leadership, the quality development staff, and the rest of the organization. This relationship is crucial for good organizational outcomes.

Quality improvement is an organizational phenomenon; therefore, your leadership role will be very important to the final implementation of any quality program. Performance improvement encompasses a multitude of organizational learning processes, and only an effective and visionary leader can make integration of these processes a pain-free process for an organization.

Through leadership participation and involvement, there is a greater possibility for the organization to develop, implement, and monitor the progress being made in the area of quality and performance improvement. It is very important for you as leader to be visible and present on quality issues in the organization and to use this presence to provide effective mechanisms and methods for planning, designing, and allocating available internal resources for quality improvement.

In recent years, we have seen both federal and state regulatory bodies asking for leadership involvement in organizational quality initiatives. According to the Center for Medicare and Medicaid Services (CMS), there can be no transformational change in the quality behavior of an organization unless the leaders within it support and promote this behavior. It is expected that leaders will make quality improvement their top priority and enthusiastically provide any leadership support that may be needed. Quality improvement in your organization will need an effective transformational leader who is ready to use his or her position to influence and encourage employee participation in a quality-improvement.

In essence, the leader must be seen as a designer, a promoter, and an enforcer. Let us look at each of these roles separately.

Designer: Your designing role includes the following.
- Setting the organization's strategic goal
- Building a framework for transparency
- Building a framework for organizational behavior that supports quality improvement
- Setting expectations around the organization's quality improvement• Assisting in the development of policies

and procedures for your quality improvement

Promoter: After you design the program, you will need to promote it—to use your role as a leader to influence others to accept your ideas and plans on quality improvement. Your promoter role will include the following actions:
- Communicating your quality ideas to your leadership team, physician leaders, and other members of the organization
- Attending board meetings to let board members know what you are doing and providing an action plan on both positive and negative results
- Attending staff, service-line, and department head meetings
- Identifying service improvements needed to sustain quality gains
- Acting as the face of quality improvement
- Using your dashboard to communicate your scores on quality indicators and data

Enforcer: Whatever you are doing, someone needs to keep an eye on it, making sure that people are doing what they are supposed to do and that customers are getting what they are supposed to get. You do this by taking the following actions:
- Creating consequences for noncompliant behaviors
- Giving support for positive behaviors and attitudes
- Making sure that the rules are applied to everybody equally
- Promoting empowerment
- Making participation in quality improvement easy and friendly
- Promoting openness and dialogue
- Demonstrating your expertise on quality with every

encounter

How else can you be a quality leader? To be effective, you need to have people working for you who are as passionate as you are about quality improvement. You don't need bench warmers on your team. You need people who understand their role and the significance of performance improvement to the organization and its customers.

You need to understand the role of your board members. You need a board that is fully engaged in your quality program. The board must be active and must assume a significant role in implementing the quality improvement initiatives that you are advocating or implementing. The board involvement can help you in the communication, image-formation, and planning that are needed when it comes to financing and allocating resources for your quality programs.

It is your responsibility to provide the necessary oversight that is required for safety and compliance. Provide a written resolution or policy on performance improvement for the organization. Help in the communication of this resolution to your leadership team, physician leadership, and all other members of the organization. Your role is also to ensure that there are policies and procedures in place that support the organization's goals on patient care. Your primary role here is to make sure that these policies are being followed in every instance of care delivery.

This may sound funny, but you need to find means of developing a working relationship with your medical staff. You need forward-looking, quality-oriented medical personnel who will help you communicate and advocate for your program to fellow physicians. The support of this group is very important for the successful implementation of your quality programs. Physician partnership is one thing you need to work on to make sure you have their support.

Review and adjust educational plans as developed by your quality improvement department. Let them feel your support for their plan on education. Find time to go over your quality indicators and patient- and employee-satisfaction data. Be proactive with action-plan development and help reinforce discipline when needed.

You need to develop a transparent culture. Your support of a culture that permits openness will be crucial for any improvement. Development of a user-friendly incident report system can solve the problem of cover-ups. This system must be communicated to and advocated for all groups, not just your clinical staff. Encouragement must be given to those who follow the rules. Let your risk-management staff help with any risk behaviors they see as troubling and make sure you participate in teaching the new behaviors.

As the person in charge, you need to increase your support for upholding the standards for product quality and customer service. Find ways of staying close to your customers. This is an opportunity for you to know how your services and products stack up in terms of quality. Make customer satisfaction your top priority. Be sure that all your attention is devoted to patients and to the quality of the services your organization is delivering.

Questions to Ask Yourself
- What do you think your role is in helping your organization to maintain quality?
- In describing your quality improvement program, which aspects of this program do you like most and why?
- How would you describe your organization's performance improvement and how are these results communicated to the frontline staff in your organization?

Behavior #10:
Embrace Diversity

The diversity goals of your organization should be not only about color and religion; they should be about inclusion, tolerance, and growth for both the organization and the individual member of the organization.

There is no doubt that today's health-care organizations consist of different types of professionals—physicians, nurses, pharmacists, laboratory technicians, social workers, and others—who contribute to care delivery. Each of these groups has its own culture and set of norms, and each member of these professions has a different cultural and educational background that must be considered before it is possible to create a productive organizational culture. This unique structure of the organization has made diversity management an issue for leadership to tackle.

If your organization is inclusive and has embraced diversity, I congratulate you, because you are on the path to organizational success. If your organization is one of the traditional non inclusive organizations, I have news for you: this is not a good situation for your organization because of the new demand by consumers and workers for a more inclusive organization.

The only way for an organization to achieve its potential and goals in today's economy is by bringing different ideas from different people into the organization. The traditional organizations may have worked in the past, but they can no longer work today. If the goal of the organization is to be more competitive, the remedy will be to look for a new process that is going to help the organization be more integrated and inclusive.

More and more people of different backgrounds and cultural orientations are looking for organizations that are prepared to work with them in their quest for a better future. We know that a culture that lacks diversity is not only bad for the organization; it is also against the law that guarantees equal opportunity for all. We also know that more diverse groups produce better, more innovative ideas than do groups of people who look, talk, and think the same.

We are seeing that minority groups are becoming more educated, intelligent, and have high expectations. They have spent time and money on themselves. They are not like an older generation of people who waited for the organization to develop them; the new generations of minority workers have trained themselves. They have struggled to get the experience that your organization will need. Ironically, most leaders lack training in how to create a work environment that allows for easy integration of this new, forceful group of minorities. Also, our organizations lack meaningful programs or tools that leaders can use to identify these people and their potential.

I like how Rumay Alexander put it when he wrote that "valuing diversity is the how-to of valuing and managing relationships, and valuing relationships is the heart of valuing and managing diversity." This statement is what I call *basic leadership rationality (BLR)*. BLR is the ability of a leader to bring every stakeholder to the table to meet the common goals of the organization. This is a unique act in leadership and management that looks at how the leader fosters unity and collaboration in the organization. BLR looks at the complex situation and how the leader utilizes this complexity to bring everybody together for the sake of the organization.

It is through good diversity-management programs in organizations— especially in the health-care industry—that the increasing demand for inclusion can be addressed effectively.

Diversity management can be used to create an environment in which people are more comfortable and feel more valued and appreciated, and it will show the organization in a better light in the eyes of its customers and the world. Hiring a certain number of minority employees is not enough if the organization has not developed a comprehensive program on inclusion and diversity. When managers are not trained on how to create and promote a diverse workforce, the rate of turnover of minority individuals will be high.

Most leaders have been trained in the importance of cultural diversity and how to use participation as a means of getting compliance from people. The current manpower shortage in health-care industries has created a diverse health-care community and calls for better diversity-management plans. The dialogue on health-care management has shifted from how to provide equal opportunity for all in order to maintain a functioning workforce to how to create a work climate in which all employees feel that they are valued for their contributions to the organization.

You, the leader, must be willing to support a program like this because your organization's competitive spirit depends on it. As I stated earlier, the face of this group has changed—they are more assertive, determined, and educated high-achievers. Dealing with them will require the following behaviors from the leader:

- The leader must, first of all, understand his or her own feelings on diversity and inclusion.
- The leader must be ready to engage in an open and honest discussion.
- The leader must know how to promote collegiality among team members.
- The leader must discourage gossip among team members.
- The leader must know how to help the team accept the unique nature of every member of the team and help the team members to mature together as a team and not as

individuals.
- The leader must be ready to fight for the team's principles and norms.
- The leader must not be a promoter of preferential treatment but instead must treat each member equally. Preferential treatment results in disloyal and unhappy employees.

I have come across leaders whose behaviors and attitudes tell a lot about them and how they feel about their team members and how they are struggling with inclusion. I have heard statements like the following: "How can I not listen to her? She took this job because she is willing to report to me alone—she is not willing to report to anybody except me"; "She likes me, and therefore I cannot let her report to another person"; or "I'd better let her report to him because of her age or intelligence." Another statement that I found funny is this one: "She will go find another job, and I don't have another person to fill the position; therefore, I need to just work with her and make her happy." All of these statements are not only bad for inclusion but they also signal a leader struggling with his or her feelings on diversity and inclusion. Any leader who places one employee above the others will have problem with team building and will be seen as showing preferential treatment toward a section of the team. These statements will not help you build a collective spirit but instead will destroy it.

The special employee will likely become so special that she will see herself as your informant and begin to tell you about others because she has come to realize that hearing about others is your cup of tea. She will become a rumor carrier, a destroyer of team spirit. She will be telling you things that are based on her perceptions or feelings that are not necessarily true.

If you have a minority on your team, this type of behavior becomes problematic for you and the team. If you don't stop this employee from being your informant, she will begin to poison your mind, your beliefs, and your perceptions of this individual. This type of employee thrives in an environment where there is confusion.

I remember a long time ago, one of my staff wanted to be my informant and tell me about others, especially employees from other parts of the region. This employee saw nothing good in these associates. She would come to me with little things, such as their uniform colors, the way they talked, their interactions with doctors, and how they behaved when she was receiving reports, etc. This behavior did not stop until I was able to talk to her and let her know that I was not interested in all her stories. I told her I would like her to talk to these individuals and let them know what they are doing wrong. My actions were too late, as some of the affected individuals who could no longer tolerate being reported for every single thing left my unit for another one. This was a big loss for our team because of the skills, experience, and the quality of care these people were known for. This is what happens when there is no tangible diversity program or when your behavior as a leader promotes preferential treatment and when you are not able to help your staff deal with their feelings, perceptions, and understanding of others, especially the individuals who represent diversity.

In another instance, we hired a new employee whose intention was to be a dominant force. To accomplish this, she told people different stories about the team members. I remember her coming to my office and putting people down, calling them names, and speaking of how others were less trained or experienced. In the back of my mind, I knew that this individual was doing the same thing to me, telling others about me, telling them what I did and did not say—going to my boss to say things that were not true about me and about other people. The unfortunate thing was that this associate had a helper, another associate who had issues with the other associates' behaviors, performance, and orientations. These two created a very toxic work environment for the other members of our team. Our leader believed all of the things she said. Because of this individual, the team fell apart, negativity took over, and dissatisfaction became very high. It was right at about this time that I began to look for another job. I was so frustrated and angry with everything I was doing; these two associates completely destroyed my joy in the job.

A diverse culture must not allow this type of behavior. The leader must discourage the behavior because of its negative impact on the team.

What do you need to know about this new group of diverse workers?

- You need to know the people you hire.
- You need to know that your support for them is very crucial for their survival.
- You need to understand that they are there to do their jobs.
- You need to understand their limitations and boundaries.
- You need to recognize and honor their achievements.
- You need to find a mentor for your diverse individuals. A positive mentoring relationship helps to shape the perception of this group by allowing them to adjust to and discover new roles with fewer problems and difficulties.
- You need to develop informal working groups and make sure they are members.
- You need to develop an open and effective communication plan: if you are the type of leader who loves to control, micromanage, or hold on to job-related information, you will have to change your style. I say this because a diverse individual working under these conditions will perceives unfairness and feel left out and

uncomfortable. The discomfort often leads to dissatisfaction, which ultimately leads to a breakdown in communication. The individual becomes Mr. or Mrs. Yes-To-Everything and stops being the thoughtful partner that you are looking for.

Creating a diversity and inclusion strategy may demand the following steps:

- It must be planned around the values and vision of the organization.
- It must be supported by your board members and your entire leadership team.
- It must be supported by a good communication plan that encourages your staff and members to ask questions in a manner that solicits information on how to work in a diverse culture. Use the communication plan to promote both integration and equality in the workplace.
- Training on diversity and inclusion strategy must be provided to all members of the organization. The training and the feedback you get from the staff will help you measure the acceptance of the program by the staff.
- Link your program with your recruitment and retention efforts. Studies have shown time and time again that good inclusion and diversity management is also a good tool for recruitment and retention. The diverse individuals are looking for an organization that will help them develop and grow to their full potential. They seek an organization where they will be productive and useful and not just a place of work.

In my previous book, *Health-Care Management: Are Social Skills the Answer?* I wrote that diversity is all about tolerance, acceptance, and personal growth. The following core principles—known as TAP—have emerged as a comprehensive model that can be used successfully by any manager or leader when trying to introduce or reinvent diversity management in the workplace.

- Tolerance
- Awareness
- Personal development

Tolerance becomes very significant when trying to manage diversity in today's workplace. Since diversity is a word that means something different to every member of an organization, it is equally important for the leaders to consider building a culture of tolerance; this should be considered a priority. Tolerance is about acknowledging the strengths and weaknesses of all members of the organization and being willing to accept them the way they are. Tolerance removes criticism, devaluation, and condescension and helps solidify diverse interests of different subcultures, beliefs, and understanding. Tolerance can provide an organization with basic functional knowledge and expertise about people and about how to build positive interdependence among various cultures. To be able to work together as a team, people must be willing to tolerate each other and create a cooperative environment in which positive relationships among diverse members are encouraged.

Self-awareness involves exploring one's knowledge of the meaning of diversity. Leaders must encourage people to examine their own knowledge. Through self-examination, people begin to discover their own biases, prejudices, and assumptions about individuals who are different from them. If there is no self-examination or awareness of one's position on diversity, there is likely the possibility of imposing one's beliefs, values, and behaviors on others, which negates the principles of cohesiveness and team building in the organization.

Personal growth through workplace diversity is possible because of the knowledge that diversity brings to the organization. Spending more time to understand other people's cultures and beliefs and what they bring to the team serves as a better way of understanding their world view. Knowing others' world views will help people interpret their relationships with others and understand how this interpretation guides their thinking, interactions, associations, and understanding of their environment. Managing diversity effectively will include personal growth and development for each member of the organization. Leaders must encourage members to devote time and resources to various aspects of learning that improve one's understanding of others and their culture. Individuals need the skills to interact effectively with people from a wide variety of backgrounds. Through personal growth, individuals will be able to collect relevant diversity skills that are needed for better relationships and team building. Individuals will be able to perform better cultural assessments, which are needed for team unification and to make more culturally sensitive issues easier to resolve. The more knowledge people are able to acquire on diversity, the better for the organization. It will help prevent stereotyping and conflicts and improve personal relationships among members.

Having a diversity plan will not only make it easier for leaders to manage effectively, it will also help position the organization as one that is flexible and conscious of those changes going on in its surroundings. It can be a good recruitment tool for the organization. Both your diversity and inclusion program could help attract more experienced and better trained and disciplined minority workers into your organization. Your diversity and inclusion program will mean better product- and service-delivery for the organization, and will also lead to improved health-care services utilization and access by minority customers and higher customer satisfaction. It will improve teamwork and communication between members and produce more engaged diverse individuals in the organization. Both diversity and an inclusion-management program that promotes workers' involvement and participation in the organization's programs and activities are important ingredients for a better and productive workforce.

Questions to Ask Yourself
- How diverse is your organization?
- What training program are you using to educate and train your members about diversity and how are you soliciting buy-in on culturally sensitive topics in your organization?
- How often do you meet with your diverse individuals? How often do you allow comments and suggestions from others to influence your perceptions of your diverse individuals?
- What do you see as an obstacle to your diversity program? Explain.

Chapter Eleven
Conclusion

In the initial stage of this book, I was not sure whether my ten leadership behaviors are actually ones that have the potential to push a health-care organization in search of high employee loyalty, satisfaction, and performance in the right direction. One question that keeps coming to my mind is Why do leaders fail to motivate and earn the trust needed for employees to follow them in their journey to excellence? What makes for high-caliber leaders who can lead an organization to reach its potential? I deliberated on these questions for a while before I was able to come up with an answer.

Leadership behaviors are like house paint that shows off the beauty of a house. They are signs and symbols of the organization that point out the direction in which the leaders are dreaming of going. The interpretations of these signs and symbols will depend on how they are positioned on the wall. Therefore, leadership behavior reflects the values and the vision of the organization. The interpretation of these espoused values and vision by the employees will depend on how leaders behave.

The ten leadership behaviors defined and explained in this book can be seen as behaviors that every organization would like their leaders to emulate and demonstrate every time they are interacting or functioning as representatives of the organization. When in graduate school, we were introduced to the following qualities of a leader and how they could help with motivation, understanding, longevity, and loyalty of the organization's members. These qualities reflect the leader's ability to consciously broaden corporate culture and the workplace environment; his ability to listen, appreciate, celebrate, motivate, and show honesty and sincerity; and, finally, the leader's ability and commitment to a diverse workforce.

It is my belief that these ten leadership behaviors are facets of the most important characteristic of all: the ability to honor and respect the people working for you. Respect means recognition of others and their contributions to the organization. Egalitarianism means viewing others as equals. Sincerity is about being sincere to yourself. Perspective should be broad and not limited to the leader's ideas. Engagement is about knowing how to work with others and engaging them for the common goal and not the individual goals. Character is about knowing your courageous ability. And, finally, leaders' respect is about tenacity and the ability to stick to one's belief by not giving up.

In a final thought, if you are wondering why you need these behaviors and what they will do for your organization, you need to look at how your people view your methods of interaction. Do they see them as logical and meaningful for their own development and growth, or do they see them leading them nowhere? Leading and learning about your organization requires your best efforts and behaviors. You have to learn how to demonstrate these behaviors to get to your final destination of good governance, loyal employees, and a productive organization.

I urge you to think about the value that these ten behaviors will add, not only to your leadership capability but also to the organization's success.

1. Knowing the culture will help you understand what is new and what needs to be changed in the organization. It will expose you to those attitudes and behaviors of your members that are not in line with the organization's values and vision.
2. Communication will promote your listening skills and will allow you to sell your agenda and not meet resistance

along the way.
3. Your visibility will show how open you are. It will bring commonality to the whole change process.
4. Your language, your good choices of words and their usage will help with compliance and encouragement.
5. It is important that your members know that safety is the thing the organization values most.
6. Demonstrating behavior that supports and promotes both customer and employee satisfaction sends a powerful message to your members on how important these things are to you and to the organization. This behavior alone can help create a better image of the organization.
7. As a leader you must set expectations on key items that must be accomplished by the organization. Setting expectations lets everyone know what their roles and responsibilities are toward the common goal.
8. A shared governance behavior shows the leader's ability to accommodate others, to share power, and lead without covering things up. This behavior will bring more people to you and improve their perceptions of you as a leader. This behavior will help you develop a better working relationship with your members and encourage them to trust you.
9. A quality leader does not sleep—he is always awake, making sure things are done right the first time. When members see this behavior in their leaders, they are happy to promote quality and take a pledge to do their best when interacting with patients or doing other things connected to quality promotion.
10. Embracing diversity helps people see you as a nonjudgmental leader who is able to lead effectively in a diverse culture that brings different people together for the common goal.

If your goal is to be seen as an effective leader taking your people to the next level, demonstrating these ten leadership behaviors will help you immensely and speed up the rate at which your goals are achieved. Your ability to create a flourishing work environment will depend on how your followers see and view your actions, attitudes, and behaviors. Your good behaviors will attract quality workers to your organization and will help foster a better organization where loyalty, satisfaction, and good performance are no longer debatable but achievable.

Bibliography

Covey, Stephen. The Speed of Trust: The One Thing That Changes Everything. New York: Free Press, 2006.

Hiscock Shuldham. "Patient-Centered Leadership in Practice." *Journal of Nursing Management,* 2008. 16, 900–04

House, Robert J.. "Path-Goal Theory of Leadership: Lessons, Legacy, and a Reformulated Theory." *Leadership Quarterly,* 1996. 7 (3). 323–52.

House, R.J., & Dressler, G. "The Path-Goal Theory of Leadership: Some Post Hoc and A Priori Tests." In *Contingency Approaches to Leadership,* edited by J. G. Hunt and L. L. Larson. Carbondale, Ill.: Southern Illinois University Press, 1974, 29–62.

Kane-Urrabazo, Christine. "Management's Role in Shaping Organizational Culture," *Journal of Nursing Management,* 2006; 14 (3), 188–94.

Maxwell, John C. The 360 Degree Leader: Developing Your Influence from Anywhere in the Organization. Nashville, Tenn.: Thomas Nelson, 2005.

O'Grady, Porter. "Creating a Context for Excellence and Innovation: Comparing Chief Nurse Executive Leadership Practices in Magnet and Non-Magnet Hospitals." *Nursing Administration Quarterly,* July–Sept. 2009; 33 (3): 198–204.

Quiello, Michael. "Always with a Safety Mindset." *United Hemispheres,* 2010.

Rumay, Alexander. "Cultural Competence Models in Nursing. *Critical Care Nursing Clinics of North America,* 2008; 20 (4): 415–21.

Scheen, E. *The Corporate Culture Survival Guide.* San Francisco: Jossey-Bass, 1999.

Senge, P. M. The Fifth Discipline: The Art and Practice of the Learning Organization. New York: Currency Doubleday, 1994.

Stubblefield, Al. *The Baptist Health Care Journey to Excellence.* Hoboken, N.J.: John Wiley, 2005.

www.ingramcontent.com/pod-product-compliance
Lightning Source LLC
LaVergne TN
LVHW020428080526
838202LV00055B/5087